Homing

Homing In

Andrew Rumsey

with a foreword by Jeremy Begbie

solway

Solway is an imprint of Paternoster Publishing,
P.O. Box 300, Carlisle, Cumbria, CA3 0QS, U.K.
http://www.paternoster-publishing.com

British Library Cataloguing in Publication Data
A catalogue record for this book is available from the British Library.

ISBN 1-900507-72-2

Cover design by Mainstream, Lancaster
Typeset by WestKey Ltd, Falmouth, Cornwall
Printed in Great Britain by
Caledonian International Book Manufacturing Ltd, Glasgow

for Philip and Elizabeth

Contents

Foreword

Millions of words wash over our lives every day, and most of them are designed for surface effect, titillating our desire for quick sensation, and forgotten in an instant. Here are words which will make you stop and dig deep into the things which matter, not by ponderous philosophy, but by asking you to take a gin and tonic at a bar, look at a map, listen to music, watch a joiner, have a cup of tea with grandad, and in all these things find a hundred suggestions of the God of Jesus Christ.

Andrew Rumsey holds together a remarkable number of threads which are often kept apart. I had the privilege of having Andrew as a student, and I am not surprised to find penetrating theological insight on every page, but it is rare to find this intertwined with such playfulness and hilarity. Here is brevity combined with depth – the poems are all the more profound for their conciseness and understatement. Here is a fierce honesty about the ragged edges of life but shot through with great gleams of hope and celebration. Here is a love of diversity, the tangible and the particular, along with an equal love of the One who holds all things together in unity.

Unlike the poet Rumsey describes in 'the poet leaves his twenties', after reading this collection you won't find you have 'acquired taste by losing touch'! Quite the opposite. You will find you are much more fully in touch, not only with the everyday world you know, but with the God who has not lost touch with us.

Jeremy Begbie
Director, 'Theology Through the Arts',
Centre for Advanced Religious and Theological Studies,
University of Cambridge

I have hoped

I have hoped
to season my life
with some salty thing
to redeem its flavour
to seize on
some saviour
who might lift the lid
and pepper the tepid weeks
of oblique midwinter
and tightly-coiled
spring

log on

misspelt Word
the world
can't read
wait while
we play
hangman
with your
near-dead
letters
desperate for
a name

Jesus caught me

Jesus caught me
picking at the
lock of my life
with the bent pin
of my intellect
'allow me', he said
and slid in
the key

He caught me
peering into the
cracked mirror
of my vanity
I saw him behind me
smiling

Jesus caught me
in my car
puzzling over a
map marked 'me'
'you are here'
he pointed
'and the map's
upside down'

I lost Jesus
in the blurring
tears of my grief
belief a dull form
that wouldn't come clear
till in bleary view
I caught him
red-handed
in the act
slowly coming
a cross

Belgian holiday 1972

at four years old
I walked round the pond
and wondered how it would feel
to fall in
through lily pad
and slimy spawn
to graze the green pool
with my hands and
hold the goldfish fascinated.
I circled the patio privately
while you all sat
sipping long drinks
speaking in cipher
lost to my watery intent.
I gathered pace and giddy logic
launched me while you spoke
as I broke the surface
back into your world

the hardware man

the hardware man
stands resolute and nothing
gets inside him
his cold facade is furniture
that he alone takes pride in
he's papered over perfectly
the places where he's peeled
his hopes are housed in half-inch ply
his passions perma-sealed

his features finely-chiselled
and his fretwork freshly sawn
he lives life on a Stanley knife edge
blunted and withdrawn
he fears his rising dampness
but your tears just prompt revulsion
the sentiments he gives
are merely displays
of emulsion

he can't admit his failures
his stresses or his strains
although beneath his undercoat
his somewhere soul remains
still any cracks he'll soon repair
as weakness makes him nervous
he'll smother them like polyfill
that stands proud to the surface

his roofing may have seen the skylight
and his loft, conversion
his central heating
may have undergone complete immersion

but if he starts to weaken
or go green around the gables
he'll sink into his ideal home
into his nest of tables

for what is there to do
so you don't catch him off his guard
but paint himself into a corner
and leave his brushes
to go hard

confession

I'm
afraid

I'm
a fraud

lost in August

gin and tonic
at the Granta
grin and bear it
at St Mary's
brave face on it
under the ash trees

dear God please
salvage this crash
of spiral-stair sin
and fling me
the grace-rope
quick

homing in

put me in my place
good God of the
maps and moments

not this nulling
nowhere nor
the nilling still
worse anywhere

simply land me
in the kneeling
somewhere
so there I
may kiss
and miss
the
worship-shape
of home

sit still gran

sit
still
Gran
so I can
remove
the
small
spider's web
spun
like jewellery
under
your
ear

the man inside

the high
street
spills
it sings
yet still
behind front
door he
lingers

for reply

knocks
until his
knuckles ring
wonders who is out

and why
he's not
invited in

Christmas wreath

in cold circus
the wild
green grips
its
beaming
berried treasure

new year's eve

here on the brink
the rink road
ahead
ready to tread
sockless the
siren snow

into the ice's
skin-smack
doubling back
on the rest
to test still
circling sin

wherein I am
a straggler
waiting to be
picked up
or picked off
hands together
thighs closed
frozen prey to
all that
lies idol

I seem all irresolute
but have seen in
a frosted frame
the mute offering of
a steamy bowl
and will yet
cloud my glasses
in its golden clasp
soup up my soul
and hold my
sides in crazy praise

secret affair

our love is like
a red, red
nose
embarrassing
and somehow
conspicuous

let's hope
we don't
blow it

musical differences

you were keen on music
I was going for a song
I said that we should meet
and you were keen to string along

I had an evening free and we agreed
how we should spend it
so you came round for coffee
and for overtures of friendship

but from the first my thirst ran dry
my loving cup was drained
I didn't realise you
had been classically trained

our common ground we never found
your view on pop was haughty
while I could barely name one
from the top pianoforte

Brahms or Grieg which is it to be?
I said I don't know which
I'd settle for McCartney
but you plumped for Shostakovich

your temperature rocketed
with Rimsky-Korsakov
mine barely rose with Berlioz
until I took it off

we rummaged through our records
but it was a waste of time
in yours I saw Debussy
what did you see there in mine?

then 'stop' you said
'exchange your pop
for my moonlight sonata'
so very blunt with Beethoven
so frank with my Sinatra

but your plea was hopeless
as our tastes were finely tuned
opinions clashed, our pan had flashed
and I slipped from the room

you shouted "you're not man enough
to tackle my Tchaikovsky"
but it was your Rachmaninov
and I had had enoughsky

so as I turned
your Handel spurned
I mused upon our plight
your overtures, my Undertones
your Bach worse than your bite

postmodern crisis

role
models
rust
status
symbols
clash
stereotypists
clatter
clear
waters
muddy
hey
buddy
can
you
spare
a
paradigm?

paddling

in high summer
reckon I might
paddle
shyly sink
slide and slink
the streamlined lichen
in greasy orbit

I might pioneer
the groaning cold
probe the globey
pebbles in their
chuckling bed
foal's legs
blushing
with buffoon
imbalance

I may
playfully fool
in Liliput let
my Canute foot
dam the dashing
brook in bluff
control
dolphin plumes
leaping like

my holiday heart
to part with
the waters and
pad the bank back
on towelled grass
yes guess I
might paddle

Newnham and Tuscany

Malting Lane smells of plums
and the greenhouse heat hugs
your legs as you lope
down for the papers
cat-warm and dozy

past musk-rose
climb back into
chianti cool as
language schools
lay in lime and pink
lapping it up on
the lawn for
Newnham you think
is Tuscany
today

to an evangelist

I sit irritable as
a cross-legged assembly boy
while the timeless gospel
ticks by unheard
by you who hector
and jab us
towards choice

with cattle-prod words
and a voice that grates
like cheese
please

all we are praying
is give peace a glance
and the good Lord
a chance to
stick his
awe in

spiritualist poem

it must
be awfully
depressing
contacting
the dead

perhaps
that's why
no one
can find
a happy medium

I who have something

I have
no cover-up
for the scandal

no blush
for the offence
or ham
pretence

no guardian
angel or
alternative
spirituality

no slick stem
for your
gushing blood
but the snatch
at his hem
as it passes

not a morsel
for your
chopstick questions
or mine

but red
hot bread
and wine

from bitter
cold nails

just the
pearls
slipped down
the sofa's side

the hiding
face
kissed
and made up

only one
torn Christ
doing justice
to you

library reunion

their glasses clicked
as they kissed
this was a surprise
they must say
and to have met
here well my dear
we simply must talk
so

over tea tales
of time's pencil marks
in the margin
hardbacked lovers
who creased their covers
with looks long lent
and soft-whispered
regret

not like today

cup of tea grandad?
I'd love one thanks
not that you can call
it tea of course
now in my day
a cup of tea really was
a cup of tea

not like today

slice of cake grandad?
yes thanks love
not that I'll be able
to digest it of course
they put so much
rubbish in it now
hardly seems like cake
not proper cake like
we used to have
you knew where you were
with a slice of cake then

not like today

the doctor sounded
helpful grandad
doctors?
I could tell them
a thing or two
now in my day if
you were sick
you really were sick
and that was an end to it
rickets, dropsy, gout
proper diseases
with proper names

not like today

you'll pop by
next Tuesday
won't you love
I expect I'll be feeling
more myself then

not
like today

the Ugley Womens' Institute

gain is loss
wisdom folly
freedom cost
lost
found
for
truth is always tension
in the grind of death is life
I must marry contradiction
find a
pretty
ugly
wife

a vicar's dozen

there are six
of us here
two clergy in
a coffee dream
four more
far more
Cranmer keen

up with the lark
out of the ark

this is an England
you barely believe
a last chancel
trip of fifties tweed

a secret six
on surname terms
who sit historic
in the candle-damp

who rise
firm as a handshake
making a present tense
with legion fears of loss
and care rubbed red
as chalice sips
in uncommon prayer
Lord open
their lips

the old testament at a glance

the children of Israel

they did it

Yahweh

the poet leaves his twenties

on leaving his
twenties (we said
that we'd write)
and trying
to make sense
of achievements
and such

the poet
discovers on
balancing the books
that he has
acquired taste
only by
losing touch

blinking locals

a Milton milkman
semi-skimming through
the newspapers

an accountant returning home
with measured steps
up the economy drive
striving
to work out the sum
of his endeavours

a Guildhall
P.A. for the day
neatly filing her nails

a backpack
compassed couple
off sexual orienteering

Mill Road bridge
in the burst-yolk sunset

a petty thief
stealing to his door
whistling used notes
checking his
face for evidence
in the car window

fitted-carpet flatness

a hospital chaplain
with the incarnation
in his buttonhole

the Sizewell
C suds
slippering
the rude skin
of a nuclear
family within
who find
the foam
so bracing

a counterfit jogger

a store detective
in pilot's shirt
hovering in beige
over the deli
whispering
savoury nothings
into his radio
hoping for trouble

a tailor in King's Parade
taking a dubious taste
of his coffee

a church youth club
in a Bourn barn
red leader
nearly over
and out
shouts
guys, guys,
come on now
guys

a stray policeman
in a street
somewhere between
Miss Marple
and
Moss Side

Wells-next-the-sea
You-next-to-me
till I'm standing
like time
standing
still

a son's trip home

a son's trip
home
still making the
heart hot
as the tiny singe
of ginger
on my
tongue's tip
while you
were baking

accident

Christ the accident
the brittle conspiracy
of time and place

the one face
in many

Christ who
could have been
elsewhere but
who happened

slight as a word
the absurd
made flesh

Christ the gaming
chance of life
its bid and
bloody irony he
who walks headlong
into disaster
under the bus
over the landmine

Christ at fault
the fool
who lodges along
earthquake plates

the mistaken
and the mistake
maker and made

Christ breaking
the agony
of choice

all saints' day

the last
leaf
left
leaves
bough bare

three spare
buds
bleed their
pointed
waxen witness
whilst
all else
around
is
falling

automatic pilate

oh the
clowning crowning
folly
to talk up
the flecks
of my faith
and play down
the woolly wash
of weakness

innocent as
a passing sentence
fudging
judging and
nudging you
into my early grave

come on in, we're closed

exploring
church
for the first
time the new
born
asks
is this room
a womb
or a
tomb?

from a curry house

a couple of newlyfeds
moan slowly
into their hot towels
whilst in the corner
a waiter dreams of laying his love
on a bed of rice
and resting his head
on her pilau

horse on the motorway

there's
a horse on
the motorway
mad-eyed
chaotic
a horse for
pity's sake
rearing at cars
jarring with
history as
hazard lit we

swerve and curse
the out of place

think though
how normal
blinkers and spurs
this horseless
carriage race

face the truth
that you're a
flapping plastic
carrier caught
high in a winter tree

half-masted man
with no fast and
no festival
flagging the M6
in a restive
disparity

oh God give integrity
in my secret heart

love is a homecoming

love is
a homecoming

an exhale
or a scale

running down
hope's hill

a full
filled heart

a wondering
whooping
oneness

a welcome
awaiting

the start

hourglass

my time is an
hourglass

I had been
bottlenecked

sucked in
like a stem

cauterised
as a paper bag
gripped at the top
inflating
waiting to
burst
into fears

but you two
have opened me out

swung the
shuttered future

and
with your cupped hands

have sung the sands
over

phoenix

and yes
the greyest
ashes do
blaze again

given this
fresh fuel
this fusing
contact made

this match from
the kindling cross
phosphorously
lamping you

with impossible
new colour

eighty-four

that which you lack
will draw you back
to where
the silence
sings

the yawning gape
the ache
and crack
become a place
of springs

St Paul in Limerick
Lesslie Newbigin

"There's a pious old lady in Malta
Whose opinions no one can alter.
If you venture to try
She'll breathe a deep sigh
And recite a few words from the Psalter."

This witty collection of limericks by the theologian, Lesslie Newbigin reflects on the activities of the inhabitants of places that St Paul may have visited.

Tom Hewitt's distinctive illustrations accompany the limericks whose subjects range from the frivolous to the serious. Whatever your taste in poetry, the delightful display of verbal gymnastics, rhymes and puns in this book are bound to amuse.

"[These delightful gems] sparkle with the humour that was such a feature of this grand old man of the ecumenical movement. He had mischievous lines playing around his lips and a puckish glint in his eyes; now that is why he could compose these lovely lines, some of which take a playful dig at the pompous and oh so orthodox and correct and the dogmatic . . . God has a smile on his face."
Desmond Tutu, Archbishop Emeritus.

"Lesslie Newbigin is not only a highly original thinker and craftsman with words but a divinely inspired entertainer as well."
Professor Robin Barbour.

"Limericks are addictive, and this delightful collection by Lesslie Newbigin is compulsive reading."
David F. Ford, Regius Professor of Divinity, Cambridge University.

St Paul in Limerick signals a departure from Lesslie Newbigin's usual style of writing. Throughout his career of missionary, bishop, lecturer and Moderator of the United Reformed Church, Lesslie Newbigin (1909–1998) wrote numerous books which explored the relevance of the gospel to different cultures.

1-900507-69-2

solway

Sing that Joke
Paul Cookson

A collection of poetry for children of all ages by poet and performer, Paul Cookson. Diverse but always entertaining, these poems cover everything from school assemblies, chewing gum, superheroes, tongue twisters, family, first kisses and much more. Lively and accessible, these are poems for children of all ages.

"High speed performance poetry where you get to shout the next line, join in the chorus and laugh till your ears go pop."
Greenbelt Arts Festival.

Paul Cookson, a poet and performer, works in schools, libraries and festivals throughout the country. His poems are widely anthologised. Recently, Paul has emerged as a leading editor of collections for children.

1-900507-79-x

solway

City of Gold
Impressions of Heaven

What will heaven be like? In his foreword J. John comments that 'heaven in the Bible is not a place in the blue beyond. Heaven is God's space; it's the full reality of God.'

City of Gold draws together visions of heaven from the writings of John Bunyan, C. S. Lewis, Adrian Plass and Phil Baggaley amongst others.

Their words are beautifully complemented by the rich and vibrant contemporary art of Steve Rigley.

1-900507-62-5

solway